T0042179

SCOOBY DOODLES!

Draw, Color, and CREATE with SCOOBY-DOO!

by Benjamin Bird

Capstone Young Readers
a capstone imprint

Published in 2017 by Capstone Young Readers,
A Capstone Imprint
1710 Roe Crest Drive, North Mankato, Minnesota 56003
www.mycapstone.com

Copyright © 2017 Hanna-Barbera.
SCOOBY-DOO and all related characters and elements are trademarks of and
© Hanna-Barbera. WB SHIELD: ™ & © Warner Bros. Entertainment Inc.
(S17)
CAPS38143

All rights reserved. No part of this publication may be reproduced in whole or in part, or stored in a retrieval system, or transmitted in any form or by any means, electronic, mechanical, photocopying, recording, or otherwise, without written permission of the publisher.

Cataloging-in-Publication Data is available on the Library of Congress website.

ISBN: 978-1-62370-811-5 (paperback)

Summary: Unmask your inner artist with this collection of more than 100 activities and drawing prompts with Scooby-Doo and the Mystery Inc. gang! Create new designs for the Mystery Machine. Draw lip-smacking snacks for Scooby and Shaggy. Color creepy clowns, ghastly ghouls, and — ZOINKS! — g-g-ghosts! Loaded with dozens of jokes and facts, SCOOBY-DOODLES is sure to solve any case of boredom.

Designer: Lori Bye

Credits: Comic Up Design Studio SL: 18-19, 30, 31, 41, 46, 71, 76, 88, 114-115; Scott Jeralds: 101, 103, 126, 139; Scott Neely, 5, 6, 9, 10, 13, 14, 75, 89, 98, 104, 110, 126, 127, 140; Shutterstock: Evgenii Bobrov, 51, 64, 80, 134, Ksenya Savva, 42

All other illustrations not listed above are credited to Warner Brothers.

Answers to page 42:

Down: 1. Poison 2. Dagger 4. Hat 5. Anchor 6. Rope 9. Hook 10. Saber 11. Rum 14. Compass 16. Flag 17. Bomb

Across: 3. Map 7. Island 8. Boot 12. Coins 13. Treasure 15. Locket 17. Barrel 18. Spyglass

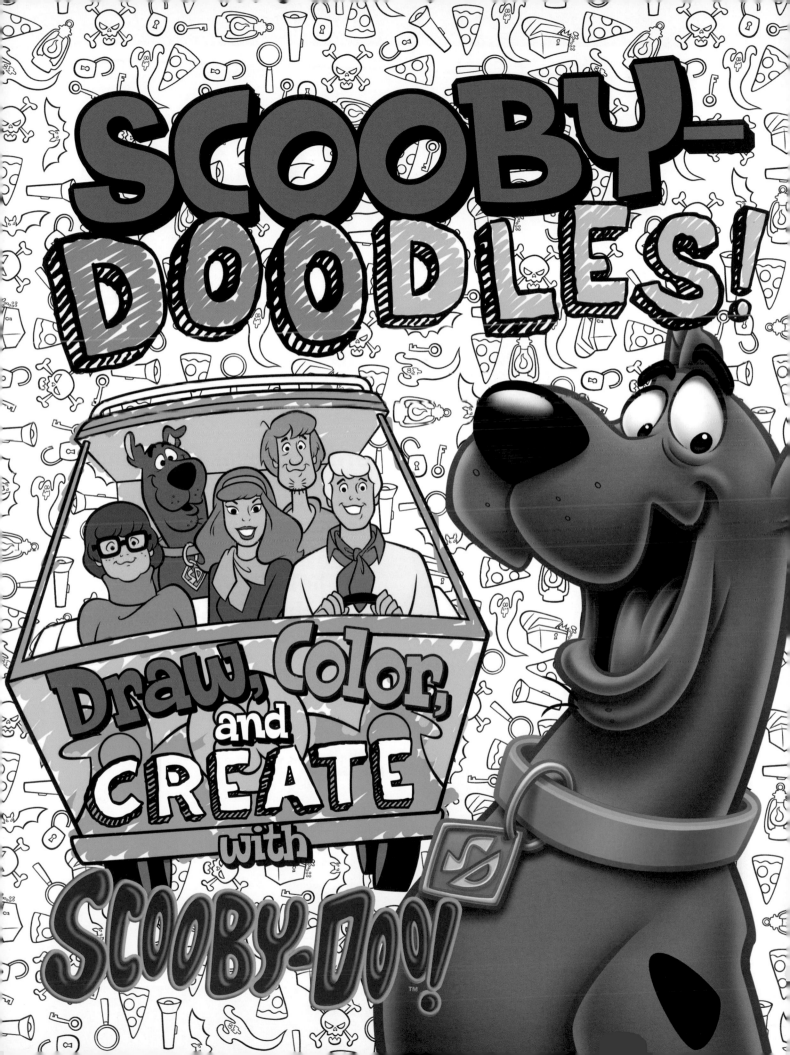

Meet SCOOBY-DOO

SKILLS: Loyal; super snout

BIO: This happy-go-lucky hound avoids scary situations at all costs, but he'll do anything for a Scooby Snack!

Follow the steps to draw Scooby!

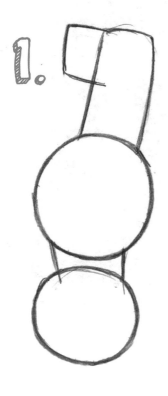

Meet SHAGGY ROGERS

SKILLS: Lucky; healthy appetite

BIO: This laid-back dude would rather look for grub than search for clues, but he usually finds both!

Follow the steps to draw Shaggy!

Meet FRED JONES, JR.

SKILLS: Athletic; charming

BIO: The leader and oldest member of the gang. He's a good sport — and good at them, too!

Follow the steps to draw Fred!

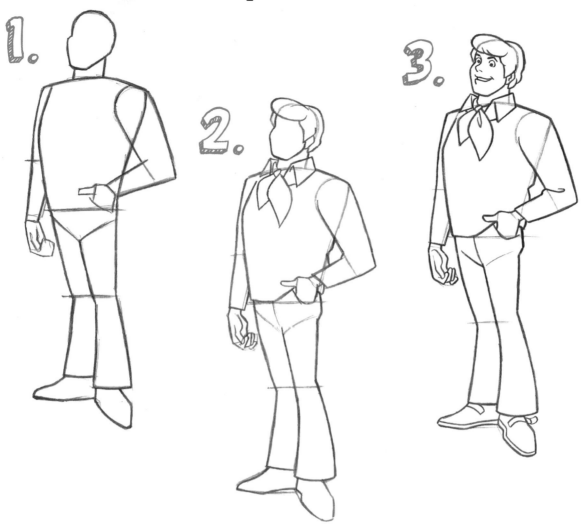

1.

2.

3.

Meet DAPHNE BLAKE

SKILLS: Brains; beauty

BIO: As a sixteen-year-old fashion queen, Daphne solves her mysteries in style.

Follow the steps to draw Daphne!

Meet VELMA DINKLEY

SKILLS: Clever; highly intelligent

BIO: Although she's the youngest member of Mystery Inc., Velma's an old pro at catching crooks.

Follow the steps to draw Velma!

Draw the MYSTERY MACHINE

This green and blue van is an important part of Mystery Inc., transporting Scooby and the gang to mysterious locations across the globe.

Follow the steps to draw the Mystery Machine!

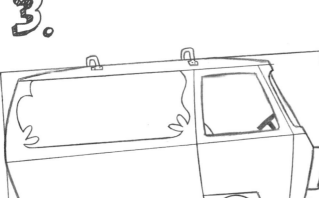

Scooby-Doo and the gang track down criminals in
THE MYSTERY MACHINE!

Give their van a far-out new paint job!

ZOINKS!

Scooby-Doo and Shaggy have a found a clue!

Draw what they've discovered.

Design six new dog tags for Scooby-Doo to choose from!

SCOOBY-DOO CAN'T SOLVE THIS MYSTERY ALONE!

Add other Mystery Inc. members to the
Mystery Machine . . . or add yourself!

RUH-ROH!

Turn the page and draw Scooby-Doo coming
out the other side!

Fill the page with more creepy eyes!

"MY GLASSES! I CAN'T SEE WITHOUT MY GLASSES!"

Doodle Velma a new pair of spectacular specs.

LIKE, Shaggy's hair has vanished!

Give him a groovy new do.

Scooby-Doo and Shaggy are on a ghost-hunting safari.
Draw a scary jungle scene behind them!

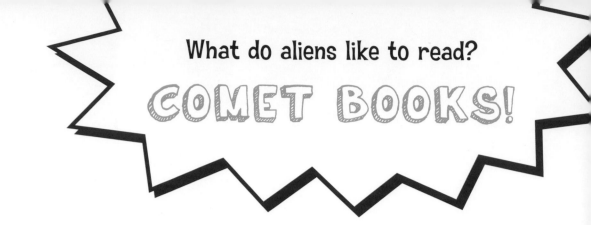

What do aliens like to read?

COMET BOOKS!

28

Doodle an
OUT-OF-THIS-WORLD
spaceship for these awesome aliens!

SCOOBY-DOO
DIGS FOR CLUES!

Draw what he's searching for beneath the ground.

RUMMY!

It's lunchtime for Scooby-Doo.
Doodle his MONSTROUS feast!

Give Scooby's name a fun new color and look!

Create stylish new scarves for Fred.

What's a PIRATE'S favorite subject in school?

ARRRRRRRT!

Doodle a pirate ship for this scurvy dog.

FEED ME!

Fill the page with more TASTY TREATS
for Scooby to eat!

SCOOBY-DOO

would go anywhere for a Scooby Snack
— even outer space!

Draw the **STARS**, the **MOON**, and the **EARTH**
around the hungry hound.

DOODLE A **HIGH-FLYING HALF-PIPE** FOR SKATEBOARDING SCOOBY!

Create a
FUNKY NEW DESIGN
for your own name!

Why won't anyone kiss Dracula?
He has BAT BREATH!

FILL THE NIGHT SKY WITH BATS!

Doodle DELICIOUS DRINKS
to quench Scooby-Doo's thirst!

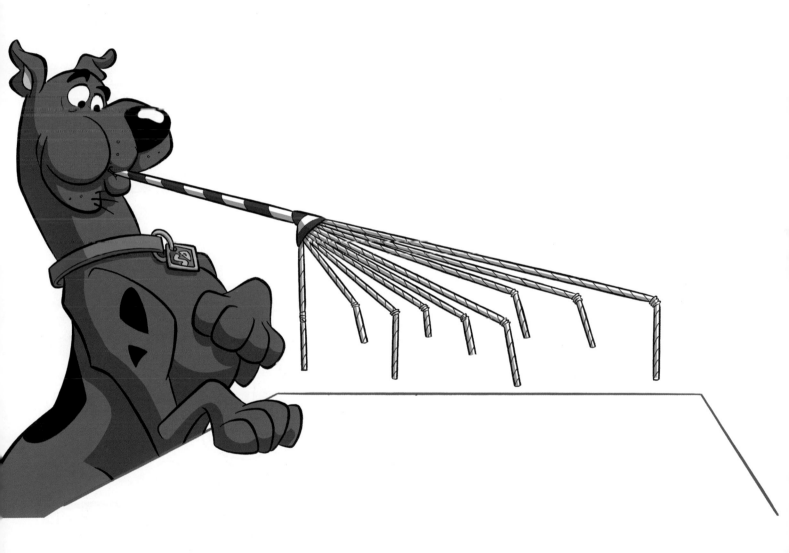

MYSTERY MAP!

Solve the crossword to complete the map!

Now try your hand at drawing your own treasure map, or WALK THE PLANK!

Draw your own Scooby-Doo monsters!

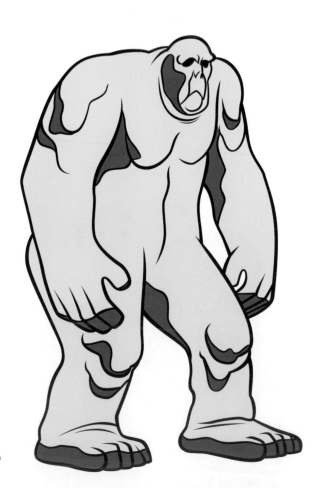

45

Fill the sky above Scooby with
BRIGHTLY COLORED BALLOONS!

Create a towering ice-cream cone to satisfy Scooby-Doo's
SWEET TOOTH!

Fill the sky with more high-flying fun!

What do you get if you cross a dog with an airplane?

A JET SETTER!

DOODLE

more mystery-solving equipment for SCOOBY-DOO and the GANG!

Mystery Machine, where are you?
Help the gang find their missing van.

START

FINISH!

THE MYSTERY MACHINE

51

What does a nosey pepper do?

GETS JALAPEÑO BUSINESS!

Add more **RED-HOT PEPPERS** to the page!

DOODLE prizes for Shaggy to WIN!

53

G-G-GHOSTS!

Decorate a
MONSTROUS TOMB
for this mummy to escape from!

Doodle some funny new hats for Scooby-Doo!

Draw Scooby's main course!

Scooby and Shaggy walk the
PIRATE PLANK!
Draw the shark-filled waters below.

SCOOBY-DOO SOLVES ANOTHER MYSTERY!
Who's beneath the mask? Draw his or her true identity.

RIKES!!

Scooby-Doo's afraid of his own shadow!

DRAW THE SCARY SHAPE.

BONE UP

on your maze-solving skills!

Color and finish the scene! Is Scooby in a jungle or on the moon? Where else could he be?

HELP VELMA...

solve the mystery of her missing half!

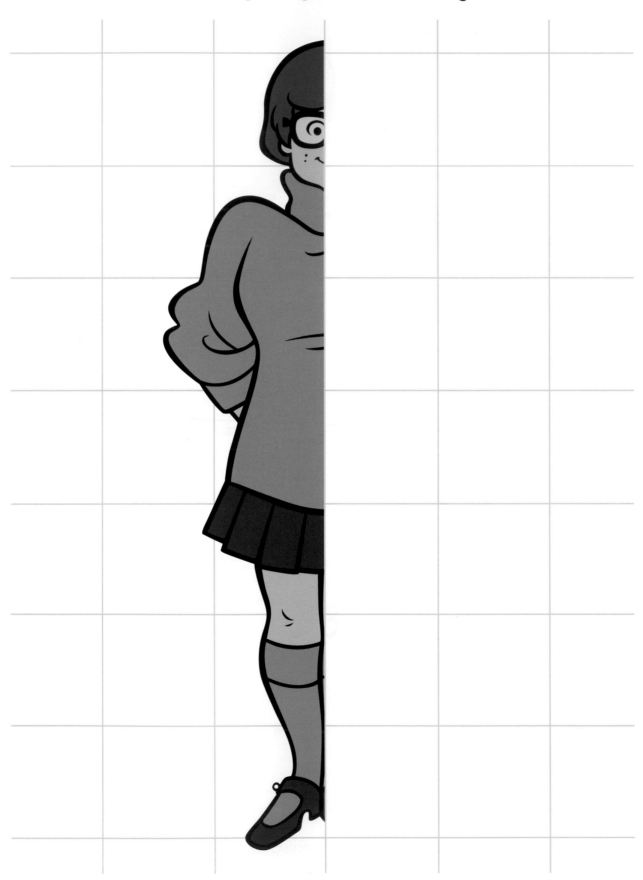

RUH-ROH!

Doodle a soft spot for Scooby to land!

COLOR THIS CREEPY CREATURE.

Decorate Scooby-Doo's
MONSTER TRUCK
with a ghoulish paint job!

X MARKS THE SPOTS!

Doodle your own pattern of spots on Scooby!

Why are jokes about circles so boring?
Because they never have a point!
HA! HA! HA!

Fill the page with more circle-shaped
pizzas for Scooby to eat!

Add GHOSTS and GHOULS
to the sky above this
CREEPY CASTLE!

Make sure Scooby and Shaggy don't get bored by the same-old Scooby Snacks. Design a new box for the tasty treats!

74

DRAW YOUR OWN BOX!

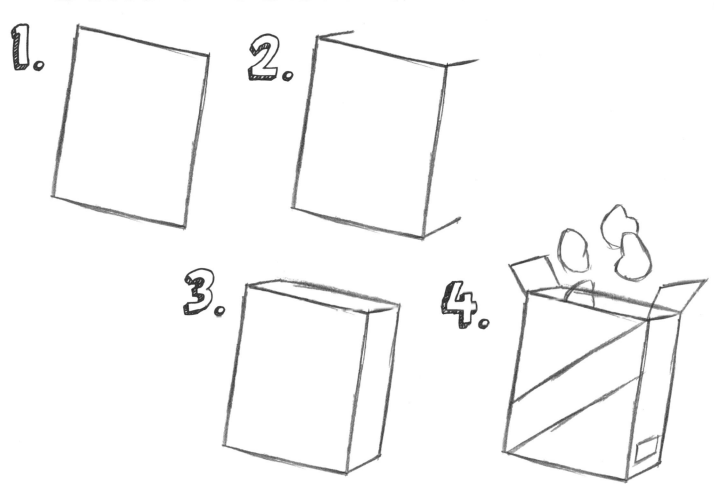

1.

2.

3.

4.

Fill the
MYSTERY MACHINE
with high-tech, mystery-solving equipment.

LIKE...HELP!

Draw Shaggy's other half.

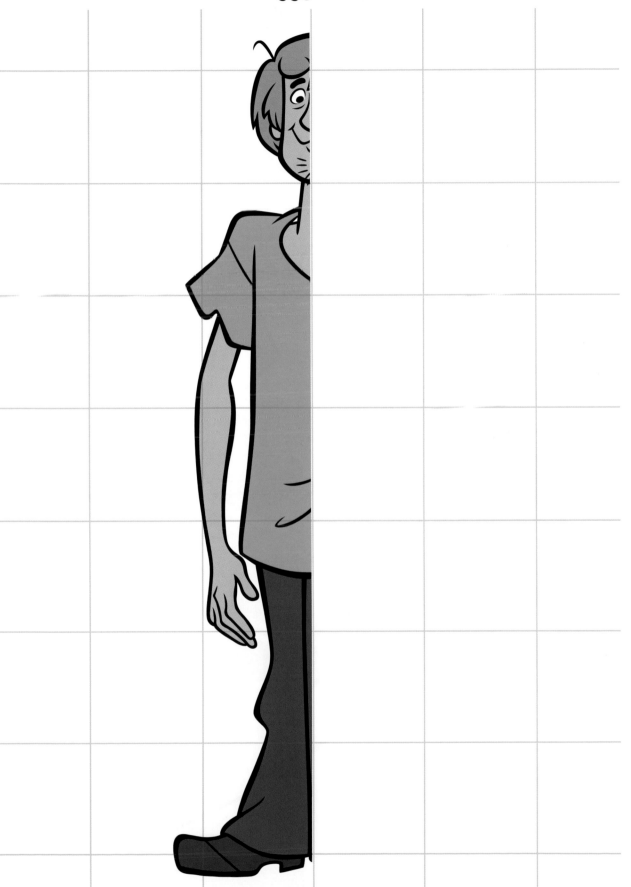

Draw the PERFECT PICNIC for SCOOBY, SHAGGY, and their OUTBACK FRIENDS.

HELP SCOOBY FIND HIS WAY TO HIS
SANDWICH!

COWABUNGA!

Create a MONSTER wave for Scooby and Shaggy to surf!

GANGWAY!!

Color the shark behind this daring duo.

GIVE SCOOBY-DOO'S HOT ROD A HIGH-OCTANE DESIGN!

Scooby-Doo loves his friends!

Create a pattern of hearts above his hairy head.

Fill Scooby and Shaggy's arms with even more food!

Help Scooby-Doo complete the face of his sculpture.

DECORATE DAPHNE'S
dress with a stylish new pattern.

Fill this stinky scene with flies!

Draw a CRYSTAL BALL
for the fortuneteller!

What will she see inside?

Give Scooby-Doo's band a name and design a logo on his drum!

Fill Scooby-Doo's dog dish with his favorite treat —

SCOOBY SNACKS!

What do you say when you meet a two-headed monster?

BYE-BYE!

Doodle Shaggy and Scooby-Doo
outrunning a two headed monster.

Why was the clown mad?
Because he broke his FUNNY BONE!

Doodle faces on the ghost clown:
scary, angry, sad, happy, silly, and more!

Create more costumes for Scooby-Doo!

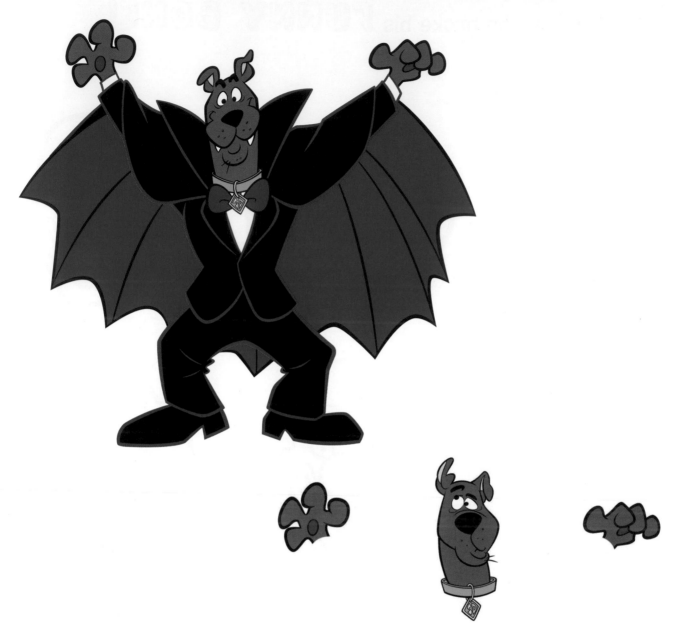

PILE MORE PIZZAS

onto Scooby-Doo's delicious delivery!

CAN YOU FIND???

```
C Z D E B Y R E T S Y M K F H D
W T O K S H A S U T K U A O K P
P O N F A D K H W U E W S M O K
K U U W I E D A A R F O C R E P
E I V U T S S G O S S S O L S M
L N A E B Z C G P K R F O E T P
Z D Z J L O N Y F C T K B A F L
O S O P K M R K D A C H Y C M W
I G G A E U A N C N A P D E B T
N R V I W G O V J S I O L R E E
K C K G H O S T K F A M F K A J
S Z O S K F K S O S O S M I S A
C Q R L N B S I R G E N A T C P
F O E B F R E D S I S W J M X T
Y L T W X A V W K I E Z U E O E
G M S S V X L N M L B A O P N C
J J N Z C S I X I O T O A A H H
P N O S Y J A L M E M T V Z K I
I Y M E I E S D A P H N E S L K
T H A S F K H S E O K M W E M I
```

Fred	Shaggy	van
Scooby	ghost	snacks
Velma	monster	jinkies
Daphne	mystery	zoinks

FLY HIGH, SCOOBY!

1.

2.

3.

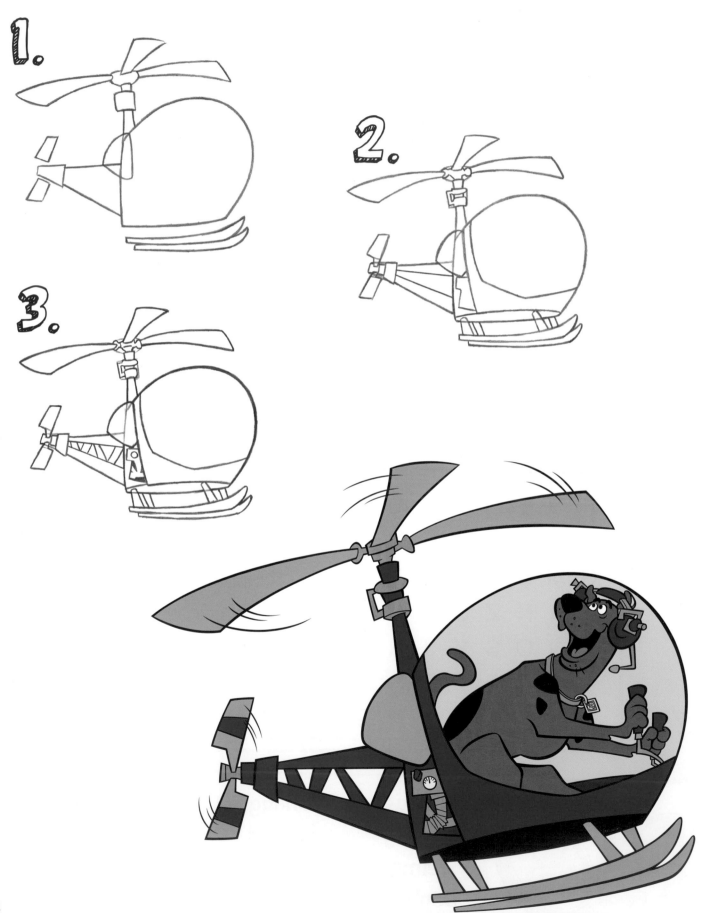

FOLLOW THE STEPS TO DRAW YOUR OWN DOGGONE COPTER!

Add monsters and beasts to this creepy forest!

Help Scooby catch a Big One!
Fill the fishing hole with MONSTER fish!

Draw even more of the many faces of Scooby-Doo!

Scooby-Doo can't stop scratching.
Cover him with more itchy fleas!

1.

2.

3.

4.

Follow the steps and give Scooby more furry friends!

Use the space below to finish this
MYSTERIOUS PATTERN!

The witch casts a

WICKED SPELL

on Scooby and Shaggy!

Doodle her magical creation.

Add a school at the end of the sidewalk!

Draw other Scooby Snack
shapes for Scooby-Doo to eat!

DRAW A YETI!

1.

2.

3.

DOODLE

an icy landscape for
the yeti to haunt!

UNMASK

THESE MYSTERY MONSTERS!

Draw their true identities.

Add even

MORE ANIMALS

to this wild scene!

Give the monster a
FRIGHTENING FACE!

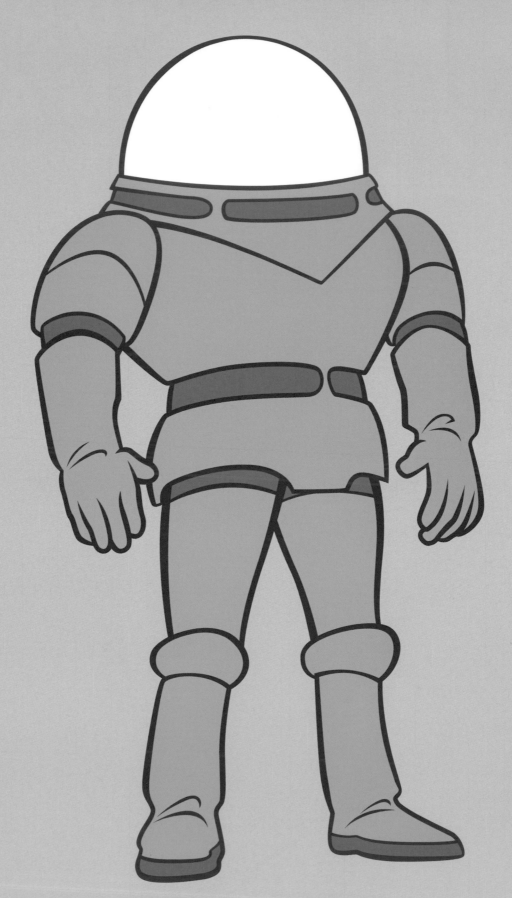

GIVE THE ZOMBIE A GRUESOME SET OF TEETH!

What mysterious artifact has Scooby
UNEARTHED?

Use your doodling imagination!

DESIGN AN OFF-ROAD COURSE FOR FOUR-WHEELING SCOOBY-DOO!

DOODLE Scooby-Doo's FANCY FEAST!

FILL THE SEA

beneath this pirate ship
with underwater monsters
and lost treasures!

RUH-ROH!

Add more Scooby-Doo paw prints to the page.

Cover the page with spooky spiderwebs!

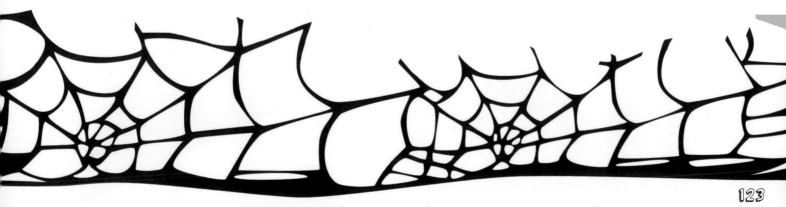

DRAW SCOOBY

ON THIS SIDE!

What do you give a sick elephant?

PLENTY OF ROOM!

1.

2.

3.

4.

NOW DOODLE YOUR OWN!

Complete the scary skull page!

Cover Scooby-Doo's favorite foods
with toppings!

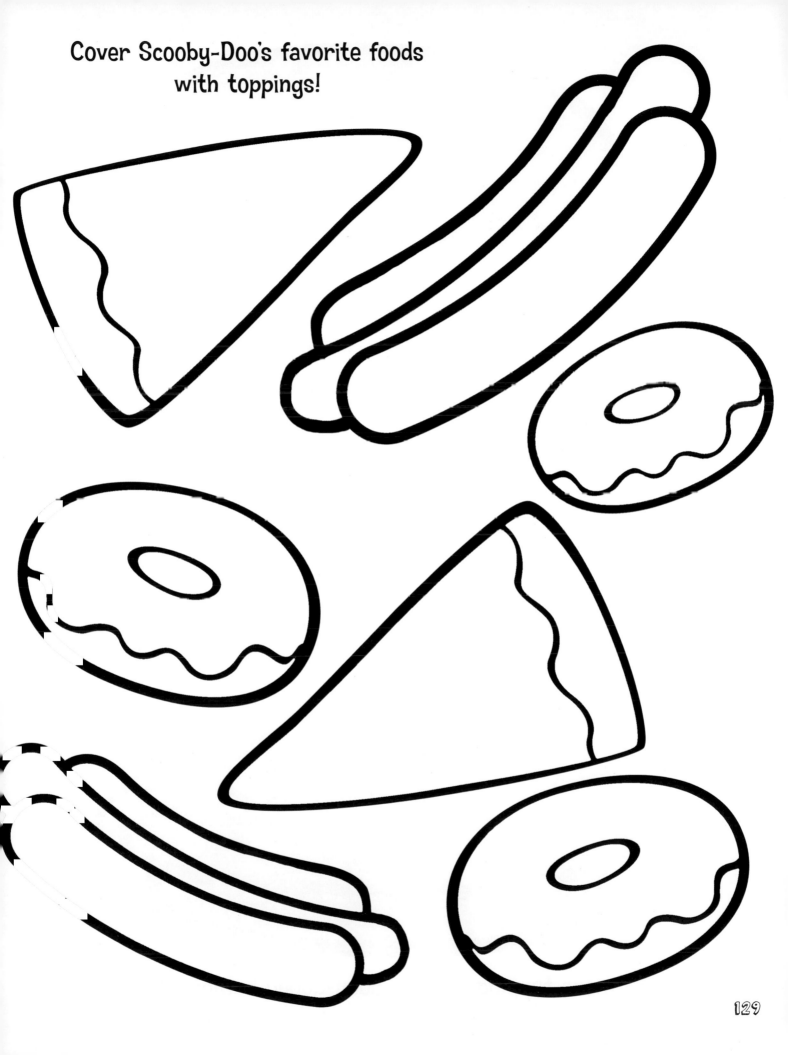

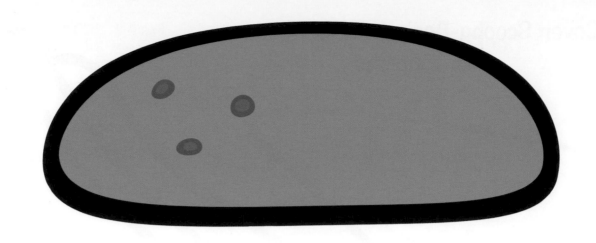

Add more toppings to this ooey-gooey hamburger!

Doodle RED-HOT FLAMES
around the fire monster!

Surround Scooby-Doo with

FLUTTERING BUTTERFLIES!

Doodle a supersized sandwich for
Scooby-Doo to scarf down!

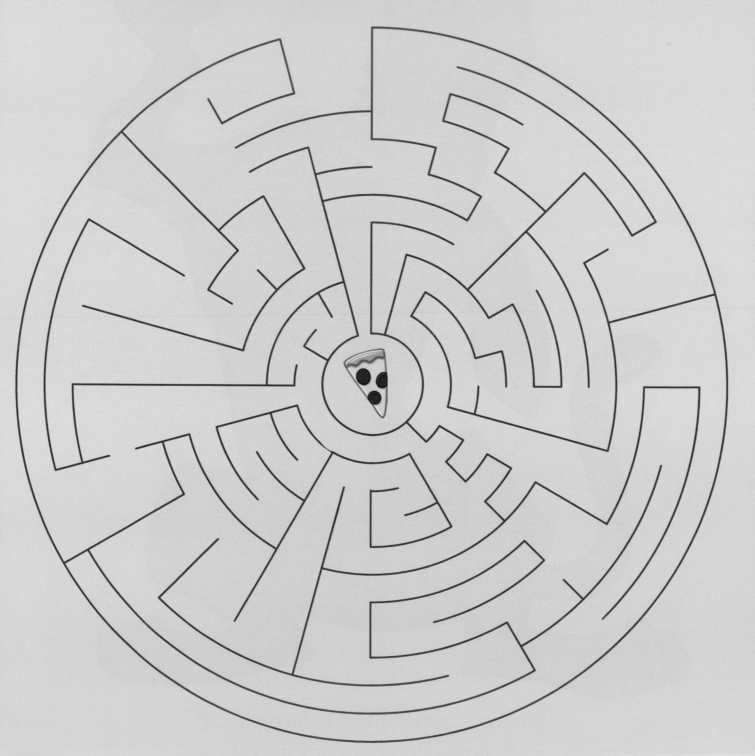

Color camouflage outfits for Scooby and his pal Shaggy.

Draw four brand-new vehicles for the gang!
Then give them each a name.

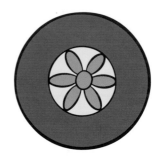

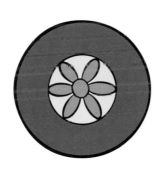

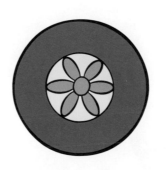

ADD MORE HOT DOG

TOPPINGS
FOR SCOOBY
TO JUGGLE!

RIKES!

Draw a scary movie for Scooby
and Shaggy to watch.

1.

2.

3.

4.

140

T. REX TROUBLE!

Doodle a T. rex chasing Scooby by following the step-by-step instructions!

CHECK OUT MORE SCOOBY-DOO BOOKS!

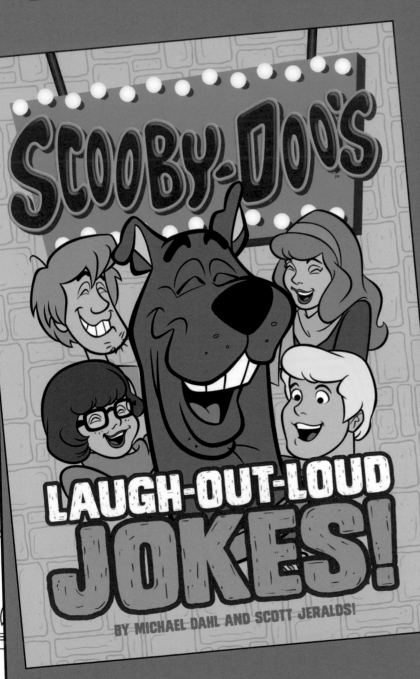

SCOOBY-DOO'S LAUGH-OUT-LOUD JOKES!

BY MICHAEL DAHL AND SCOTT JERALDS!

← YOU CHOOSE →

SCOOBY-DOO!

THE MYSTERY OF THE AZTEC TOMB

POSSIBLE 13 ENDINGS

by Laurie S. Sutton

← YOU CHOOSE →

SCOOBY-DOO!

THE MYSTERY OF THE MAZE MONSTER

POSSIBLE 10 ENDINGS

by John Sazaklis

← YOU CHOOSE →

SCOOBY-DOO!

THE GHOST OF THE BERMUDA TRIANGLE

POSSIBLE 12 ENDINGS

by Laurie S. Sutton

Time for a
NAP!